BIGM

Morrissey

CW00686830

PAT REID

To Sharron from the German Vegan Oliver.

Sept. 1998

THE DUNCE DIRECTIVE

Contents

G E N I

p E a N g I

Death

18

TION BY JOHN PEEL A

U ₅ S

EX ⑨

MONEY 26

BIGMOUTH introduced by John Peel

It was through John Walters that I first heard of Morrissey. Walters had been to one of the early Smiths gigs and came back very much impressed, saying, "Hey, we've got to book this band" – which is something he rarely does. Shortly afterwards I met Morrissey on *Round Table* and enjoyed the way he so obviously delighted in delivering his splenetic views of other people's records. He was motivated more by the desire to impress than by the holding of any heartfelt beliefs for or against any particular record. It was certainly better than the kind of banal nonsense we usually got.

I bumped into him again when I was driving down from Edinburgh having annoyed some students by playing records they didn't like. I stopped at the services just south of Newcastle and was sitting there having a cup of tea when he came over, said hello and then to my astonishment announced that this was his favourite motorway service station! I think that was taking pickiness a bit too far because never in all my life – and I'm a man who likes to make lists – have I felt a need to make a list of my favourite motorway service stations. Doubtless, after reading this the next Morrissey Fanclub convention will be held in that very same service station.

In a way I find the uncritical adoration of 'the star' rather sad and with Morrissey it does have a strong sexual element. *I'm* pretty uncritical about The Fall but I don't fancy any of them. Nice kids and all that, but I wouldn't want to shag 'em. If The Fall made a bad record then frankly I wouldn't know because so long as it's them and Mark E. Smith can be heard carolling away, then I'm entirely happy. So I understand a certain amount of that, I understand the musical aspects but not the intense personal adoration.

Ultimately, the adoration is rather destructive to people's art. You can't function properly, function creatively, if you're adored. I remember somebody once writing about Tiny Tim, "Tiny Tim, once a universe, now a star". In a way I think that's what has happened to Morrissey.

G E N I U S

Manchester, 1984. A teenage schoolgirl sets eyes on a lanky figure
familiar from magazine covers and Top of the Pops. Dressed in
Levi's and a plain shirt, with an already-famous quiff perched on
top of his head, it is Morrissey, singer with The Smiths. Plucking
up her courage, she eventually summons the nerve to approach the
palely loitering singer.

"Aren't you that Morrissey?" she blurts breathlessly. "Why do
you stick flowers in your pocket?". Stooping slightly, the six foot
singer looks at her. Charming, polite, he speaks:

"Fuck off, little girl."

The anecdote is an appropriate introduction to Morrissey, not
least because it's as apocryphal as the rumour once spread by the
Inspiral Carpets that Britain's most famous vegetarian had been
sighted enjoying a burger in MacDonalds. True or not, the tale il-
lustrates some key themes in the ongoing saga of one of pop's most
controversial figures.

Primarily, Morrissey is a pop star who remains, in a sense, ap-
proachable. He lives in Primrose Hill after all, not Beverley Hills.
Scenes at his 1991 London shows confirmed him to be the one star
who permits 'mere' fans to invade his personal space, to kiss him

and touch him. Yet, paradoxically, he remains a mystery. In this role he succeeds David Bowie, who has gone to extraordinary lengths in a personal demystification revealing him to be -gasp- just as mundane as everyone else. Morrissey is still holding out on that account. While he might allow his audience to reach out and touch him, he is also keeping a great deal hidden and, like the little girl in the story, those who attempt to probe further are often dealt with in an alarmingly brusque manner.

Few writers who have interviewed Morrissey in person have managed to avoid falling under his spell. Those who try to dig deeper, however, are met with swift resistance from the Morrissey camp and over the years the closed ranks of his inner circle have come to resemble a Masonic lodge rather than a popstar clique. As far back as 1985 when rock writer Nick Kent was researching a Smiths feature for *The Face*, he received an anxious call from the group's 'ersatz manager' Scott Piering:

"Ah, Nick, I really don't quite know how to broach this because, well, I'm convinced you're an ally and you've clearly put a massive amount of thought and research into your story but, erm, that's why concern is so rife."

A bemused Nick Kent was compelled to disclose the written results of his enquiries among Morrissey's old Manchester acquaintances. Kent's innocuous spadework had alarmed the singer and as he explained, "I am very concerned about what they said because at least one of them is a sworn enemy who would get no small quotient of pleasure from wilfully misinterpreting my activities, I'm afraid to say."

Morrissey's jealously guarded privacy was once more threatened, with the publication of Johnny Rogan's investigative biography *Morrissey and Marr – The Severed Alliance* (1992). The project had been in preparation for four years, involving painstaking research and even some co-operation from its subjects, but Morrissey immediately issued a vicious denunciation. A spiteful missive was forwarded to the *NME* wishing for Johnny Rogan's death in a motorway pile up.

In fact the only person who has been close to Morrissey and written about it in any detail is Sandie Shaw, the '60s singer whose career Morrissey helped to revive in the '80s. Her 1991 autobiography *The World At My Feet* offers brief but fascinating observations of Morrissey the 'real' person but, as is so often the case with those once close to Morrissey, the two appear no longer to be friends.

Despite his high-handed behaviour, Morrissey remains a unique and fascinating figure. With The Smiths he revitalised rock music in the '80s, achieving critical and commercial success. As a solo performer his success continues, although his love affair with the UK music press comes nearer to breaking point with each successive release.

Morrissey's dealings with the press completely dominated a number of publications during the '80s. The coverage afforded him traversed extremes of worshipful fawning and venomous abuse because, like the public, the press have a problem with Morrissey – problem being: you either love him or hate him.

Before ill-founded accusations of racism caused a barrage of controversy in August 1992, Morrissey was singled out for more pleasing attention as sole cover star of the 40th anniversary edition of the *NME*. This accolade highlights the relationship between Morrissey and *New Musical Express* which has provided the most intriguing saga of star/media interaction in the history of British popular music. Although the paper had successfully made the transition from covering '70s progressive rock to chronicling the punk explosion, its identity during the '80s became inextricably linked with The Smiths and in particular Morrissey. When its writers were raving about hip hop and the new forms of dance music, its readers wanted little except The Smiths and sub-Smiths fare such as The Housemartins and The Wedding Present. A change simply had to come, and come it did, taking the form of a backlash of epic proportions. The Smiths almost killed the *NME*, but in the end the *NME* killed the Smiths. Allegedly Morrissey still blames the paper for the group's demise. Editor Danny Kelly's choice of 40th anniversary cover star, however, could not have been more apt: *"To our knowledge, no-one else quite sums up the paper over the past ten or so years. Rarely has a pop personage and his relationship with a music paper produced so many sparks, so much debate, so much excellent copy, and (ahem) so many yards of Angst."*

Morrissey has always had many detractors but his enduring success is undeniable. With around thirty hit singles (including those credited to The Smiths) and ten albums comfortably reaching the UK top ten, he stands alongside Prince and Madonna as one of the most prolific hitmakers of the last decade. Certainly his sales fall well below the likes of Madonna, but this is partly due to his resolutely indie approach to stardom.

Quite apart from record sales Steven Patrick Morrissey remains the brightest star we've got. True, it is lamentable that nobody has quite managed to succeed to office the man once described by *Sounds* as the "NUM Leader of Pop". Morrissey is a hard act to follow and the shadow cast by The Smiths' music on '90s rock is comparable to the legacy bequeathed to the '80s by the Sex Pistols.

So what is to be said of the camp crooner of Stretford, Manchester? He was born on May 22nd 1959, making him roughly the same age as Madonna, Prince and Michael Jackson. He is as famous for his avowed celibacy, his vegetarianism and his support for animal rights as for his music. His angst-ridden adolescence is notorious, as are his obsessive devotions to Oscar Wilde, James Dean and Sandie Shaw. His zealously protected private life contrasts wildly with his flamboyant live performances and the hysteria they inspire in people who don't usually get hysterical about anything other than general elections and the price of Doc Martens. He may be many things but of one thing you can be certain: Morrissey is sexy.

EX

What price Morrissey's sexuality? Ever since the early days of The Smiths, when he first claimed to lead a celibate existence, speculation has been rife. Certainly no lover has ever initiated a kiss-and-tell scandal, so we may assume there have been no lovers. With so many of his personal heroes either homosexual (Wilde), bisexual (Dean) or completely ambivalent like Edith Sitwell and the New York Dolls, it seems appropriate to place Morrissey in the sphere of the sexually ambiguous pop star, along with Bowie at his most androgynous and Jagger at his most dangerous.

Morrissey's professed celibacy remains one of the most powerful and subversive elements of his overall image, especially nowadays when Bowie and Jagger would rather stay home with the wife. The real importance of the consistent allegations of celibacy has nothing to do with whether the claims are true or not but everything to do with the *idea* of celibacy itself. Morrissey can never be just another rock star chasing his dick around the gossip columns. It is the *idea* of celibacy that sets him apart.

Despite this he retains a fascination for the murky depths of the human condition, and observations of other people's sexual rituals are common throughout his work. This is evident in the first Smiths product, *Hand In Glove*. The implicit sexual overtone of two people fitting each other like a hand in a glove together with the naked male buttocks adorning the cover helped set the scene for much of what was to follow.

Hand in glove
the sun shines out of our behinds
The good life is out there, somewhere
so stay on my arm, you little charmer
But I know my luck too well
and I'll probably never see you again

The lyrics suggest an unreal quality to the relationship. The joy fades like a daydream and the note of desperation seems to suggest a fleeting homosexual assignation, conducted in haste and secrecy, never repeated.

It has often been noted that throughout Morrissey's lyrics the narrative voice is usually so shrouded in obscurity that it becomes difficult to determine matters such as gender: "Suedehead *could be about almost anyone – himself, his mother, a male or female lover – little is revealed apart from a sense of personality and sensitivity.*" (*NME*, 20th Feb. 1988) While Morrissey's humorous material tends to have a very clear storyline (e.g. *Vicar in a Tutu*, *Get off the Stage*), making sense of the sexual element in the lyrics is near impossible. Generally, however, the Morrissey persona is the passive partner in sexual transactions:

Meet me at the fountain

shove me on the patio
I'll take it slowly
(*Reel Around the Fountain*)

So how do we reconcile Morrissey's avowed celibacy with the sexual awareness and earthy sensuality of his lyrics? As James Brown commented in the NME (Feb. 11th 1989): *"I find it hard to believe that it is a Crown Prince of Celibacy who is responsible for such knowing or flirtatious songs as* Late Night, Maudlin Street, Reel Around the Fountain, Hand in Glove *and* Alsatian Cousin. *Or for the specifically sexual visual control of his image, from the last topless* NME *front cover to the particularly lustful dancing of the young tearaway hoodlum on the new video."*

Morrissey's response to this scrutiny is to declare that his obsession with the minutiae of sexual matters has arisen precisely because he has never had any sexual life of his own. In the same interview he suggested that a person who was genuinely promiscuous and sexually hyperactive would probably be more interested in writing about anything other than sex.

Returning to the factor described by James Brown as Morrissey's 'specifically sexual visual control of his image', it must be said that the projection of male sexuality, in pop generally, provides an ugly commodity. Morrissey has allowed a relatively simple image to work for him, whilst infusing the medium with a degree of wit and originality. The pop stars with the most enduring sexual image are those who employ strong, simple visual elements. Marilyn Monroe and James Dean are pop stars in the true sense with their eternal influence over pop culture, while Sinatra, Elvis and Madonna are also good examples. Like David Bowie, Madonna is a frantic image-hopper, but the two are at their best when their styling evokes classic themes. His premature death ensured that James Dean is permanently frozen in the image of his early twenties. Morrissey has made use of that same image for ten years. The basic compo-

nents of denim jeans and a quiff are a 'look' from which he rarely departs. Despite his mock aggressive stance, James Dean was sexy because he was relatively unthreatening, and Morrissey has successfully utilised Dean's essential aura of decency and sensitivity. The image also owes something to Montgomery Clift (and British counterparts Laurence Harvey and Dirk Bogarde) who slipped from icon status simply because he got older, dying at the unhip age of 46. Morrissey endeavours to combat the ageing process by staying the same.

In the '80s, Morrissey's sexual image and the chemistry of The Smiths were similar to other successful pop groups, notably the short-lived megastars Culture Club. In his book *Like Punk Never Happened: Culture Club and the New Pop*, Dave Rimmer looks back to the role played in the '60s by homosexual managers of pop groups. The self-assured swagger of The Beatles was, to some extent, "the cool, cocky brashness of a kid who'd found himself a sugar daddy and got set up in Mayfair". Culture Club were a New Pop prototype, nodding to this time-honoured tradition but with a difference, in that everything took place within the group itself. Boy George's relationship with Jon Moss, the band's drummer and driving force, is curiously similar to the crucial partnership of Morrissey and Johnny Marr in The Smiths. Dave Rimmer pinpoints a key factor in Culture Club's visual presentation, describing a typical group photograph:

"George will stand surrounded protectively by these three hunky men pouting and grinning into the camera while they look as butch as possible. His expression says one thing: 'Look what I've got, girls!'" On the sleeve of *The Queen Is Dead*, Morrissey's air of self-contentment as he poses with Johnny, Mike and Andy outside the Salford Lads' Club recalls Boy George's coquettish antics. This visual gambit continues to this day, most notably with the gang of sexy toughs led by Morrissey in the promo for *We Hate It When Our Friends Become Successful*. Had James Dean been in a band then doubtless they would have looked like Morrissey's 1992 roundup of rockabillies and rebels.

It is worth noting that in the '80s Morrissey was a mainstay of pop press publications like *Smash Hits* and *No 1*, which had no trouble at all in accepting his offbeat persona. This was, after all, the age of outlandish specimens like Boy George and Pete Burns (with whom Morrissey enjoyed a brief friendship). That Morrissey identified so readily with these high priestesses of camp is unsurprising, given his widespread gay following. In the music fanzine *Outlook* (Jan/Feb '92) Mark Simpson observes that the overwhelming attraction of Morrissey is the fact that many Morrissey fans, whilst not quite filling the role of 'skinheads with nail varnish' which the singer once envisaged, are nevertheless a clan of soft-hearted ruffians lifted straight out of Morrissey's songs. The air of liberation that fuels hysterical scenes at his concerts is unleashed by Morrissey's challenge to the essential hardness of conventional male values:

"For them (the fans) Morrissey expresses the hitherto inexpressible: masculine sensitivity and inadequacy. Moz allows them to live because he allows them to feel – and so they love him."

Morrissey's appeal to women remains a curious phenomenon. His concerts attract mothers, daughters, the overweight, the unattractive, the despairing and the very beautiful. There is a smattering of lesbian support, which considers him both sympathetic and politically sound. He enjoys the friendship and admiration of the outspoken lesbian singer Phranc, and songs like The Smiths' *Half A Person* (from *The World Won't Listen*, 1987) take a sympathetic glance at lesbianism.

Morrissey has always been vocal in his admiration and support for women and feminism, and perhaps in this context his challenge to conventional male values lends its support to unconventional female values. In *The Smiths* (1985) writer Mick Middles attributes Morrissey's awareness of the Women's movement to a volume he read in his teens entitled Men's Liberation. Another important influence was Linder, singer with the group Ludus, Morrissey's alltime favourites from the golden age of Manchester punk. It should also be remembered that it was his mother (often viewed as a formidable figure, divorcing her husband to bring up the young Steven alone) who introduced him to much of the literature that was to prove so important later.

Women also featured as cover stars for many Smiths releases, from the portrait of Pat Phoenix on the *Shakespeare's Sister* single, to the Alexandra Bastedo sleeve on the *Rank* LP. Since his solo career began in earnest in 1988, Morrissey's sleeve designs have been given over to narcissistic self images, but with The Smiths, the cover artwork was a more peculiar and unique expression of his talents. Although cover stars like James Dean and Elvis have become cultural cliches (no matter how potent they remain), such figures as Pat Phoenix and Viv Nicholson are inspired choices as home-grown additions to the pantheon of sexual icons. By comparison, the homoerotic statements, such as the Joe Dallesandro sleeve of the debut album, are safe and ordinary – nothing new to Warhol aficionados. The female cover stars (Pat Phoenix, Yootha Joyce, Billie Whitelaw) are peculiarly English and almost second hand in their appropriation of glamour. They tend to hark back to Morrissey's childhood favourites and must have been central to his evaluation of adult sexuality.

Those classic sleeves, while establishing a corporate identity for The Smiths, often generated trouble. The most notorious amongst such incidents was in June 1984 when major retail outlets banned the *Heaven Knows I'm Miserable Now* single, objecting to the B-side, *Suffer Little Children*, mistakenly assuming in some quarters that the cover star was 'Moors Murderer' Myra Hindley. The beehived blonde in question was in fact Viv Nicholson of 'Spend, Spend, Spend' notoriety. Nicholson became a household name in 1961 when, as a young miner's wife, she won the pools and embarked on a spending frenzy in pursuit of happiness. In many ways Vivian Nicholson remains the archetype of all that Morrissey holds dear. She is unashamedly working class, yet upwardly mobile; extrovert with an appealing tang of glamour and tacky sexuality, a streetwise yet sympathetic character who has seen it all and done it all and had it all and lost it all. In addition, Nicholson is eternally lodged in Morrissey's preferred landscape of '60s nostalgia.

For a man so fascinated with people and their behaviour it seems remarkable that Morrissey is apparently incapable of forming a sexual relationship. It is interesting that in his lyrics any hint of sexual love is invariably darkened by the shadow of violence and death. Even in the more comic moments – *especially* in the comic moments – sex and love are inextricably linked with pain and cruelty. Songs such as *Sweet and Tender Hooligan* and *I Want The One I Can't Have* highlight Morrissey's obsession with violence and criminality and his earliest awareness of these themes must date from the '60s when the crimes of the Moors Murderers terrorised the working class streets of his childhood. It is possible that Morrissey's celibacy is linked to these horrific local events, and that he has grown up to associate sex with torture, murder and violence.

Nick Kent's 1985 Morrissey feature for *The Face* airs the conviction that the crimes of Myra Hindley and Ian Brady had a profound and far reaching effect on the seven year-old Steven Morrissey. He told Kent: *"I happened to live on the streets where, close by, some of the victims had been picked up. Within that community, news of the crimes totally dominated all attempts at conversation for quite a few years. It was like the worst thing that had ever happened, and I was very, very aware of everything that occurred. Aware as a child who could have been a victim. All the details you see, it was all so evil; it was, if you can understand this, ungraspably evil. When something reaches that level it becomes almost absurd really. I remember it at times like I was living in a soap opera..."*

Many years later Morrissey was still coming to terms with the Moors Murders, and one of the earliest lyrics he proffered to Johnny Marr was eventually to become *Suffer Little Children*, a mournful elegy to the victims and their families.

In the Morrissey milieu, love, like sex, is equated with violence, pain and death.

If the Smiths reached a pinnacle of emotional intensity on *The Queen Is Dead* LP then *I Know It's Over* on side one, along with side two's *There Is a Light That Never Goes Out*, are the most poignant of Morrissey's twisted love songs. The former embodies all the lyrical elements which by 1986 had become virtual Moz cliches.

The story is old but it goes on – the snivelling Steven has lost his 'sad veiled bride' to a 'handsome groom' and a 'loud loutish lover.' The cliches abound, but never before had Morrissey made them work for him to achieve such emotional impact. His greatest strength is the ability to express mundane everyday woe and this is perfectly conveyed by the numb self-realisation of the lyric:

if you're so funny, then why are you on your own tonight?
and if you're so clever, why are you on your own tonight?
if you're so very entertaining, why are you on your own tonight?
if you're so terribly good-looking, then why do you sleep alone tonight?
because tonight is just like any other night
with your triumphs and your charms, while they are in each others' arms

This desolation is belied by the soaring hopefulness of *There Is A Light That Never Goes Out*. Again the song contains prime Morrissey cliches: the car journey representing freedom, the sense of alienation from the people at home, and the clumsy fumbling in the 'darkened underpass'. In Morrissey's most evocative love song the violence of the imagery is ludicrous and ludicrously moving:

and if a double decker bus, crashes into us
to die by your side, such a heavenly way to die
and if a ten-ton truck, kills the both of us
to die by your side, the pleasure and the privilege is mine

The Queen Is Dead stands as a unique, classic album. Its prevalent themes are Morrissey's pet loves and hates: the comic, the tragic, the politic and the downright odd. Which brings us to the hit single *Bigmouth Strikes Again* (number 26 in the UK charts in June '86). For many this was an introduction to the thoroughly distasteful humour of The Smiths:

Sweetness, sweetness I was only joking
when I said I'd like to smash every tooth
in your head
Sweetness, sweetness I was only joking
when I said by rights you should be
bludgeoned in your bed

Morrissey takes a common occurrence and sends it way over the top, playing the Ortonesque black comedy for all it's worth.

If *Bigmouth* depicts domestic violence in a relationship, then *Girlfriend In A Coma* is a sequel of sorts. The girlfriend has ended up in intensive care (why? – because her boyfriend carried out the threat of Bigmouth to smash every tooth in her head?) and the narrator can't bring himself to see her, even though he realises 'it's serious'. Despite the jaunty arrangement and the calculated shock value title the song isn't played for laughs. Instead it's a sensitive portrayal of a person undergoing deep trauma. Morrissey uses the flat hollow phrases that may be heard from any accident victim to express a true sense of loss:

there were times when I could
have 'strangled' her
(but, you know, I would hate
anything to happen to her)
Would you please
let me see her!

Do you really think
she'll pull through?

In Morrissey's world Love is always contaminated with the suggestion of violence. Even the motherly love of *Suffer Little Children* and *The Hand That Rocks The Cradle* exists solely as a protection from the lurking cruelty of life:

my life down I shall lie
if the bogey-man should try
to play tricks on your sacred mind

Unsurprisingly there are few straight love songs in Morrissey's oeuvre. The closest The Smiths get to it is with the boppy *Sheila Take A Bow* (UK number 10, April '87) which equates the thrill of love with sheer ecstatic joy, while exhorting the Sheila of the title to 'boot the grime of this world in the crotch, dear' – as if Morrissey could get through a set of lyrics without perpetrating at least one random act of violence. Another batty love song opens the track listing of the US Smiths compilation *Louder Than Bombs*. *Is It Really So Strange?* sees Morrissey 'getting confused', killing a horse and sending a nun the way of all flesh, before the real horror sets in and he loses his bag in Newport Pagnell. As usual, the quantity of his love is gauged in terms of how much punishment he can take:

Oh yes you can kick me
and you can butt me
and you can break my spine
but you won't change the way I feel
'Cause I love you

In refusing to write straight, positive love songs, Morrissey has not only gone against the grain, but created a whole new genre.

The accepted vocabulary of pop remains extremely limited, but before Morrissey a hit single like *Girlfriend In A Coma* would have been unthinkable. Anything similar would have been the preserve of country & western or of novelty 'death songs' popular in the '60s and *definitely* not something to be taken seriously. It is precisely this ability to challenge the lightweight nature of pop music, while retaining a deft pop sensibility, which makes him unique.

For Morrissey the real and symbolic significance of death is enormous. Violence and death are referred to either implicitly or explicitly in almost all of his songs. Illness, disability and death are favoured interview topics; suicide and gallows humour are mainstays. Certainly a number of his songs can be described as, well, deathly, but these moments are counterbalanced by the stomping, surging, uplifting and comic elements. Detractors have always found Morrissey ludicrously depressing but, paradoxically, the overwhelming fervour of his live audience ignites reserves of great vitality. Morrissey doesn't fear death: he flirts with it, talks of it teasingly, surrounds himself with reminders of its inevitability and, finally, emphatically reaffirms that he is alive. The crowd members who run across the stage towards him mirror this ethos en masse.

Paint A Vulgar Picture from *Strangeways Here We Come* (1987) sets a grim scene. A pop star has died and the record company clamours at the prospect of bumper profits. Often viewed as a thinly veiled attack on *Rough Trade*, The Smiths' label, the song actually concerns the way in which death is marketed. As Morrissey explained to the NME in February 1988: *"It was about the music industry in general, about practically anybody who's died and left behind that frenetic, fanatical legacy which sends people scrambling. Billy Fury, Marc Bolan..."*

With its anguished sense of adoration *Paint A Vulgar Picture* implies that premature death ensures everlasting fame. Morrissey is drawn to those such as Dean and Bolan, whose untimely termination enables them to remain eternally young and hip in pop culture

heaven. It's a powerful idea, though ridiculous, and Morrissey expresses it with the righteous passion of blind fan worship. In *Paint A Vulgar Picture* the lone fan mourns unnoticed, representing Morrissey mourning Bolan, but also resembling a certain kind of Morrissey fan who desperately wishes for his hero to die in a plane crash before he stops being cool.

If Morrissey equates love with violence, he also juxtaposes the certainty of life with the anticipation of death. His preoccupation with death is surprisingly refreshing in the context of pop music. Although TV, film and literature, as well as real life, are drenched in death, pop songs that treat the subject with intelligence or humour have always been rare. *Death Of A Disco Dancer* (1987) later seemed prophetic after increased clubland violence in Manchester during the early '90s, while Morrissey's hopes to release *Stop Me If You Think You've Heard This One Before* as a posthumous Smiths' single were dashed when the BBC objected to the song's casual reference to 'mass murder'.

Death is also used to force home political beliefs. The point of *Meat Is Murder* is that the deaths of animals also matter. The song is necessarily a dirge, its truths unpalatable: *A death for no reason and death for no reason is murder.*

By comparison *Margaret On The Guillotine* (1988) is positively lightweight. The year after the third consecutive Tory election victory Morrissey implored his listeners to execute the prime minister. Not the most subtle piece of political commentary (nor indeed much of a song), but a nice idea.

Ouija Board, Ouija Board (1989) was widely greeted as proof of Morrissey's spent talent. In hindsight it's a gem, a perverse novelty record, gleefully at odds with the trends of the time and ironically, far less ridiculous than those trends appear now. Attempting to contact a deceased friend, Mozza flirts with the occult, a realm usually reserved for the morbid pantomime of heavy metal. However, the pathos of the lyric, and the appearance of Carry-On star Joan

Simms in the video injected a dose of camp quirkiness into proceedings. Steven makes contact with his dead chum, and is told to push off, sending himself up with some charm.

Morrissey's interest in death is perhaps best expressed by his outspoken views on euthanasia. Suicide has been a submerged factor in Manchester pop ever since Joy Division singer Ian Curtis killed himself in 1980. Although The Smiths claimed to stand against the 'greyness' that Joy Division supposedly typified, many would find them an equally depressing alternative. Illness and depression are lyrical mainstays, with suicide close behind, sometimes light hearted, sometimes not.

Asleep (1987) is innocent enough at face value, with it's wintry atmosphere, music box effects and 'sing me to sleep' refrain. At once tear-jerking and chilling, it expresses the desire to go to sleep and never wake up, simultaneously pathetic and strangely dignified. Morrissey has always claimed to respect and sympathise with those who choose to take their own lives and has admitted to having been in correspondence with the families of several suicides. After the Smiths' split there were reports of distraught fans committing suicide, prompting the NME's acid remark, *"It's when they get back together that the suicides'll really start."*

The suicide factor enhances Morrissey's status as a cult figure in the true sense of the term. That a tiny minority is so obsessed with him that killing themselves becomes a means of expressing some spurious solidarity underlines disturbing aspects of the Morrissey persona. After the assassination of John Lennon the widowed Yoko Ono found herself issuing pleas to fans not to commit suicide. As one of The Beatles Lennon was, as he infamously remarked, bigger than Jesus.

Morrissey is small fry by comparison, but the fervour he inspires is peculiarly intense. There are those, it seems, who will follow him unquestioningly, and death does not appear to be a major deterrent.

MONEY

'*Fame, fame, fatal fame, it can play hideous tricks with your brain,*' he sings in *Frankly, Mr Shankly* (1986). True words indeed, although spoken in jest. Fame has changed Morrissey, as if being revered and despised with equal passion by media and public, and having fans top themselves whenever the line-up is reshuffled wouldn't change anyone. In the early days of The Smiths Morrissey was everywhere, interviewed by all the magazines, appearing on TV and radio. After the Smiths split he retreated beyond the public gaze. The lid on his private life closed tighter than ever, and few interviews were forthcoming. When he does speak to the press he remains controversial but is increasingly isolated from prevailing trends in the music scene.

Projects that stray into the bounds of the singer's privacy, such as the Johnny Rogan book, are met with hostility, while actions such as the last-minute cancellation of appearances at Finsbury Park and the 1992 Glastonbury Festival seem to signify a disdainful attitude towards the fans.

Regarding Morrissey's isolation there are two schools of thought: those who think he remains in isolation in order to stay sane and those who think it's because he's gone mad. Certainly he surrounds himself with a nigh-impenetrable circle of intimates who inspire the bitchy in-jokes of *Certain People I Know* (1992) and *We*

Hate It When Our Friends Become Successful (1992). It has always been expected of Morrissey that he should shun the conventions of rock'n'roll – the sex and drugs, the alcohol and petty crime. On another level he is perhaps more aware of the fundamental myths of rock'n'roll than anyone. This is reflected in the obsession with fame, which rivals even his excessive interest in death. A premature death would guarantee him everlasting fame but one assumes he is too shrewd to fall into the sad 'rock death' trap of Sid Vicious or Johnny Thunders.

The isolating effect of fame on a pop star inevitably leads to accusations of selling out, and the likelihood that new recorded material will be lyrically irrelevant to the original fan base.

In The Smiths Morrissey's themes were poverty and desperation, but his imagery never pretended to provide a realistic portrayal of contemporary life. He has always belonged to the past. Indeed his enthusiastically received *Your Arsenal* (1992) takes its lyrical themes and musical motifs from the 1970s. Morrissey's dilemma of credibility is not quite the same as the rapper who continues to talk about guns, gangsters and ghettos long after having upped and moved to Beverley Hills. In any case, despite his fame, Morrissey has consistently and persistently grappled with issues that affect all of us.

He does himself few commercial favours with his outspoken views on animal rights, euthanasia, and the Conservative Party. However, the no compromises attitude has often paid off. *Meat Is Murder* (1985) sent an animal rights statement to number one in the UK charts, displacing the cheeseburger rock of Bruce Springsteen. *Viva Hate* (1988) also a number one, contained *Margaret On The Guillotine*, which called, without the least trace of irony, for the execution of the then Prime Minister. *Panic* (1986) also called for blood, the blood of crass Radio One deejays who played pop dross while Chernobyl burned.

Two singles from the period of Morrissey's critical nadir dem-

onstrated his willingness to sacrifice commercial gain for the sake of uncompromising subject matter. *Interesting Drug* (1989) was released at a time when almost every hit single contained puerile submerged references to the recreational drug ecstasy. While music fans turned on to the escapism of rave culture, Britain was entering a recession that would make the one that spawned The Smiths look like a tea party. *Interesting Drug* looked at the 'young married couple in debt', high and dry 'on a government scheme designed to kill your dream', taking drugs not for cheap thrills but through desperation. These were the people who couldn't afford the ticket to a rave, whose names weren't on the guest list. The lyric suggests the '80s heroin epidemics of cities like Liverpool and Edinburgh. Though softly tuneful, Morrissey was talking about the hard stuff.

November Spawned A Monster (1990) took another taboo subject into the top twenty, namely disability. Critics found the subject distasteful and the song tuneless. They were wrong on both counts. The arrangement is reminiscent of Jacques Brel or Nick Cave in its darkly passionate delivery, the vocal is superb, and the words are among Morrissey's finest, describing a disabled girl victimised by a supposedly caring society:

Jesus save me from
pity, sympathy
and people discussing me

Fame is a big business and Morrissey is part of it. A notoriously capricious recording artist and performer, his business dealings reveal that many people have been trampled beneath the unstoppable Morrissey machine. Of the four members of The Smiths only the song writing duo of Johnny Marr and Steven Morrissey actually held a contract with *Rough Trade*. In effect Morrissey and Marr were The Smiths and, despite their enormous contribution, bassist Andy Rourke and drummer Mike Joyce were in legal

terms little more than session musicians.

An equally crucial part in Morrissey's career was played by former Smiths producer Stephen Street, who provided the music for *Viva Hate* (1988) and much of *Bona Drag* (1990). The dissolution of this partnership was caused by a disagreement over money. The dispute arose when Street's solicitor contacted Morrissey's representative requesting that they settle the question of Street's unpaid US royalties before proceeding with new recordings. Street had a production deal with *EMI* for the UK and the rest of the world but Morrissey product was handled by *Sire* in the States and no agreement had been drafted to include Street, "*And this was a good year after* Viva Hate *had come out,*" Street told *Outlook* in 1991. "*Morrissey must have took it that I was trying to screw him. So Morrissey being as he is wrote me a very cryptic letter saying 'Enough is too much' and that was it – I was cut off.*"

Astonishingly, at the scene of one of Morrissey's greatest triumphs, the 1988 Wolverhampton concert, his entire band comprising ex-Smiths Mike Joyce, Andy Rourke and guitarist Craig Gannon were in the process of suing the singer for monies owed. At the time it seemed odd that Stephen Street, though a gifted musician, did not perform the songs he had written and played on *Viva Hate*: "*Again, I felt a bit pushed to the side there because it was the ex-Smiths type thing. I don't think they were very happy about my joining them. I think they were hoping it was going to turn into a big Smiths reunion, perhaps get the thing going again. I felt slightly out of the gang.*"

As prima donna extraordinaire Morrissey is adept at playing off his supporting cast members against one another. Sandie Shaw witnessed this phenomenon at first hand during the *Viva Hate* recording sessions:

" *'I can't tell you how much I love them all,'* Morrissey gushed in an unaccustomed expression of deep affection. (He was later to have one of his radical changes of heart and blow them all out.) They all seemed

deeply in love with him too. It was intriguing to observe each vying with the other for his attention, his laughter, his approval or his admiration of their musical prowess. They tiptoed around in his presence as if on eggshells, not wanting to offend their maestro." (The World At My Feet, 1991).

Working with the maestro proved too much for Johnny Marr. In an *NME* interview six months prior to the Smiths split, Marr was sounding increasingly fragile, continually referring to the 'pressure' of life in The Smiths. Johnny Rogan's controversial *Morrissey and Marr: The Severed Alliance* (1992) examines Marr's predicament in detail, revealing that the guitarist felt trapped in a group in danger of becoming an anachronism. Business matters also helped bring things to a head with Morrissey stubbornly refusing to cooperate with manager Ken Friedman, who enjoyed good relations with Marr.

Morrissey himself is no stranger to the pressures of fame. On the surface he appears to be coping, typically avoiding the traditional avenues of escape for a star – drink, drugs and so forth. On the other hand, it's a simple matter to view his behaviour as that of a madman. His media-baiting pronouncements, his wilful artistic and business conflicts all bear the signs of an increasingly unbalanced mind. Or do they? Morrissey is a pop star who in recent years has been deemed unfashionable by a previously fawning press. However, he has continued to maintain a high level of coverage. How can this be, if he is really so washed up, so artistically bankrupt, so old fashioned, and if in any case the readers no longer have any interest in his doings? Patently, demand for Morrissey remains high. He does what pop stars are supposed to do; he generates publicity.

All this attention grabbing has its downside. In an *NME* feature from February 1989 James Brown observed the singer at his home near Manchester, besieged by obsessive fans who hung around to ring on his doorbell, waiting glumly for them to go away and leave him alone.

BIGMOUTH: a decade

Morrissey started 1992 on the cover of the *NME*, and ended it on the cover of *The Observer Magazine*. His television appearances commenced with a performance on *The Late Show*, introduced by motherly arts commentator Sarah Dunant, and concluded with a breathtaking display on the prestigious US *Saturday Night Live*, compered by bemused *Batman* actor Michael Keaton. Clearly he was attempting to go upmarket and mainstream simultaneously. He may just succeed.

Although a triumphant year, 1992 was also fraught with scandal. *Your Arsenal* gave him his highest ever US chart placement, while in the UK he chalked up three hit albums – *Your Arsenal*, and the Smiths compilations *Best 1 & 2*. *Best 1* went to number one, confirming The Smiths' status as one of the greatest rock groups of all time. Morrissey will doubtless shoot himself in the foot a few more times but his current career as living legend has him nestling comfortably with Lou Reed and Scott Walker in the closet reserved for perverse geniuses.

The Finsbury Park fiasco cast a shadow on what might otherwise have been a perfect year. His brief appearance draped in a Union Jack along with the track *The National Front Disco* from *Your Arsenal* led to swift accusations that the singer was flirting with extreme right wing views.

Race has been an issue with Morrissey before. In 1986 the line from *Panic* 'burn down the disco, hang the blessed DJ' was inter-

preted by some as an attack on black music. It was left to an honest, earnest Johnny Marr to clean up the mess; "*Violence is disgusting but racism's worse and we won't deal with it.*" Nowadays Morrissey answers such questions himself, but his ambiguous replies can be disheartening. In December 1992 he told *The Observer*, "*The phenomenon of the National Front interests me, like it interests everyone. Just as all manner of sexuality interests everyone. That doesn't mean that you necessarily want to take part.*"

Songs like *Bengali In Platforms* (1988), *Asian Rut* (1991) and *The National Front Disco* (1992) cannot truthfully be described as racist. *Bengali* is unintentionally patronising and insensitive, and *Asian Rut* is a touching love song to a doomed victim of racist violence, expressed in Morrissey's quaint, unfashionable idiom. In addition, it seems strange that, if Morrissey is indeed a screaming Nazi, that instead of embracing him, the National Front chose to bottle him off the Finsbury Park stage. More Adrian Mole than Oswald Mosley, Morrissey remains ever the outsider in the present day.

In spite of his conflicting public images Morrissey's cultural value is undoubted. Strangely his influence is more obvious in comedy than in music. Comedians like Vic Reeves, Rob Newman and Steve Punt sing his praises while the brilliant Sean Hughes based an entire TV series around the 'Morrissey fan' persona. What Alice Cooper is to Wayne's World, so Morrissey is to new British comedy. Perhaps he will become a megastar in America, perhaps he will remain in Primrose Hill and be Britain's top light entertainer. Or maybe he *will* die in that de rigeur plane crash. He has never sold records by the million and probably never will, but anyone who owns one of his records would argue passionately on behalf of its significance. Maybe he should get a life, or a manager even, but Morrissey will continue to provoke, inspire and infuriate for the foreseeable future.

END